SECRETS TO MAKE POSITIVE CHOICES

STRATEGIES FOR ACHIEVING YOUR GOALS

DR. JAGADEESH PILLAI

|| Dedicated to all wisdom seekers around the World ||

॰

Contents

Contents

PRAYER

"Om Bhadram Karnebhih Shrunuyaama DevaahBhadram Pashyemaakshabhiryajatraah SthirairangaistushtuvaamsastanoobhihVyashema Devahitam YadaayuhSwasti Na Indro VridhashravaahSwasti Nah Pooshaa VishwavedaahSwasti Nastaarkshyo ArishtanemihSwasti No Brihaspatir DadhaatuOm Shantih, Shantih, Shantih"

The literal meaning of this mantra is: OM. O Gods! Let us hear auspicious words from our ears. O reverent Gods! Let us behold propitious visions from our eyes, let our organs and body be stable, healthy, and strong. Let us do that which is pleasing to the gods in the life span allotted to us. May Indra, inscribed in the scriptures, bring us fortune! May Pushan, the knower of the world, grant us prosperity! May Trakshya, who vanquishes enemies, bestow us with blessings! May Brihaspati bring us success!
OM Peace, Peace, Peace.

About The Author

Dr. Jagadeesh Pillai is a renowned Guinness World Record holder, writer, and researcher hailing from Varanasi, also known as the abode of Lord Shiva. With a Ph.D. in Vedic Science and a range of creative ideas and achievements, he is a true polymath. He is the author of more than 100 books including Research Publications. Although his roots can be traced back to Kerala, the people of Varanasi hold him in high regard and affectionately consider him one of their own.

In 1998, Dr. Pillai was offered a job at Banaras Hindu University, but he left the position after only two months to pursue greater goals in life. He believed that in order to study Indian scriptures and engage in other creative endeavours, he needed to retire from the daily grind of working solely for money at a young age.

He started an export business from scratch, using the knowledge he had gained from a previous job in the industry. His intelligence and unique approach to business led to great success in a short period of time, earning him more in just a decade and a half than he would have in a lifetime working in a government job. Upon the passing of Dr. APJ Abdul Kalam, Dr. Pillai decided to leave the business and dedicate himself to reading, studying, researching, and experimenting.

During his tenure in the export business, Dr. Pillai traveled to over 16 countries, gaining valuable insight and experiencing the world and life in detail.

Dr. Pillai has achieved four Guinness World Records in the following subjects:

"Script to Screen" - In this record, Dr. Pillai produced and directed an animation film within the shortest time possible, breaking the previous record set by Canadians. He has also received numerous national and international awards and recognitions for this achievement.

Longest Line of Postcards - For this record, Dr. Pillai created a line of 16,300 postcards on the occasion of the 163rd anniversary of Indian Postal Day. The event also included a questionnaire about the Indian flag.

Largest Poster Awareness Campaign - Dr. Pillai designed an awareness campaign on the subject of "Beti Bachao - Beti Padhao" (Save the Girl Child - Educate the Girl Child) to achieve this record.

Largest Envelope - In tribute to the Indian Prime Minister's "Make in India" initiative, Dr. Pillai created a 4000 square meter envelope using waste paper to achieve this record.

Attempted - **70000 Candles on a 210 kg Cake** - To celebrate the 70th Indian Independence Day, Dr. Pillai attempted to light 70,000 candles on a 210 kg cake, which was recorded in World Records India.

Attempted - **Documentary on Dhamek Stupa of Sarnath in 17 Languages** - Dr. Pillai attempted to create a documentary on the Dhamek Stupa of Sarnath, dubbing it in 17 different languages. The result of this attempt is currently awaiting confirmation from the Guinness World Records.

Dr. Pillai is skilled in teaching the Bhagavad Gita, a Hindu scripture, and is popular among young people. He has helped many young people improve their lives through his motivational teachings.

In addition to teaching, he has composed and sung numerous Sanskrit Bhajans and patriotic songs.

He has also written and directed several short films and documentaries for awareness campaigns, and has volunteered with the police in both UP and Kerala to spread awareness about various issues through videos and photography.

Incredibly, he has produced and directed over 100 documentaries about the city of Varanasi, all on his own.

He has also helped and guided more than 25 boys and girls to achieve world records through creative and innovative methods. He is a multifaceted person who uses his intellect and the blessings given to him by God to excel in various areas. He is both a teacher and a student, always learning and teaching, and is able to master any subject he comes across.

He is a selfless social activist and motivational speaker who has overcome struggles and failures to become a successful and enthusiastic individual with a rich life experience.

In addition to his work with the Bhagavad Gita, he is also an efficient Tarot card reader, Astro-Vastu consultant, and a talented singer and composer. He has sung the entire Ram Charita Manas and Bhagavad Gita in his own compositions, and has sung the phrase "Lokah Samastha Sukhino Bhavantu" in 50 different languages. He is currently working on a detailed and scientific study of Vedas, Upanishads, Puranas, and the Bhagavad Gita. He has also composed and sung the Hanuman Chalisa and Gayatri Mantra in 108 and 1008 different compositions, respectively.

Awards - Four Times Guinness World Records, Winner of Mahatma Gandhi Vishwa Shanti Puraskar, Mahatma Gandhi Global Peace Ambassador, Kashi Ratna Award, Dr. APJ Abdul Kalam Motivational Person of the Year 2017, Mother Teresa Award, Indira Gandhi Priyadarshini Award, Bharat Vikas Ratna Award, Udyog Ratna Award, Vigyan Prasar Award, Poorvanchal Ratn Samman.

PREFACE

Achieving one's goals is a journey that requires careful planning, dedication, and hard work. However, even the best-laid plans can be hindered by negative choices and self-doubt. That's why we've written "Secrets to Make Positive Choices: Strategies for Achieving Your Goals." This book provides a comprehensive guide to making positive choices that will help you achieve your goals and live a fulfilling life.

The road to success is often littered with challenges and obstacles, and making positive choices is key to overcoming them. Positive choices create a ripple effect, leading to greater opportunities and a more satisfying life. By making positive choices, you can achieve more, learn more, and grow more.

This book is designed to help you identify and overcome self-limiting beliefs, set SMART goals, build a support system, manage your emotions and stay focused, learn from failure, and build mental and physical strength. We'll also explore the power of positive thinking and gratitude, the importance of self-care, and the role of mindfulness in making positive choices. Additionally, we'll discuss overcoming procrastination and staying motivated, building positive choices in the face of adversity, learning to adapt and be flexible, and the power of persistence and determination.

Whether you're just starting out on your journey or you're well on your way, "Secrets to Make Positive Choices: Strategies for Achieving Your Goals" is an invaluable resource. The strategies and techniques presented in this book will help you make positive choices, achieve your goals, and live a life of purpose and fulfillment. So let's get started!

I

Understanding Positive Choices and their Impact on Achieving Goals

Making positive choices is an important aspect of achieving personal and professional goals. Positive choices are deliberate actions that help you move forward in a productive and meaningful way, leading to greater fulfillment and satisfaction in life. These choices can be made in a variety of areas, including personal relationships, career, health, and finances, among others. When you make positive choices, you are taking control of your life and setting yourself on the path towards your desired outcomes.

One of the key benefits of making positive choices is that it enables you to develop a positive mindset and cultivate a growth mindset. When you focus on positive outcomes and take action to achieve them, you start to see the world in a different way. You become more confident in your abilities and start to believe that anything is possible with the right approach and mindset. This, in turn, helps you to develop a greater sense of resilience and perseverance, as you are able to overcome obstacles and setbacks along the way.

Another important factor to consider when making positive choices is the impact that these choices have on your overall health and well-being. Positive choices are often associated with healthier lifestyles, including regular exercise, a nutritious diet, and engaging in activities that bring you joy and fulfillment. These choices can help to reduce stress levels and improve your mood, leading to a better overall quality of life.

Positive choices can also have a significant impact on your finances. By making wise decisions about how you spend your money, you can put yourself on the path towards financial stability and independence. This can help to reduce stress and anxiety associated with financial difficulties, allowing you to focus on your other goals and priorities.

In addition to the benefits outlined above, making positive choices can also help you to build stronger relationships with others. When you are proactive about making positive choices, you become a better partner, friend, and colleague. You are able to create a supportive network of people who are there for you, which can help you to achieve your goals and overcome any challenges that arise along the way.

Making positive choices is an essential part of achieving

your goals and leading a fulfilling life. Whether you are focused on personal or professional goals, the choices that you make every day have a profound impact on your success and well-being. By developing a positive mindset, focusing on your health and well-being, and building strong relationships, you can set yourself on the path towards a bright and successful future.

*"The choices you make today determine the
life you live tomorrow."*

☙

II

Identifying and Overcoming Self-Limiting Beliefs

Self-limiting beliefs are negative thoughts and attitudes that hold us back and prevent us from reaching our full potential. They are deeply ingrained in our subconscious and often go unnoticed, but they can have a profound impact on our ability to achieve our goals and lead a fulfilling life. Self-limiting beliefs can take many forms, including negative self-talk, low self-esteem, and a lack of confidence. If left unchecked, these beliefs can become a barrier to success and can prevent us from making positive choices that lead to growth and success.

One of the first steps in overcoming self-limiting beliefs is to identify what these beliefs are and where they come from. Often, self-limiting beliefs are rooted in our past experiences and the messages that we received from others as we were growing up. For example, you may have heard comments like "you're not good at math" or "you'll never be able to do that" from a teacher, parent, or other authority figure, which can shape the way that you view yourself and your abilities.

Once you have identified your self-limiting beliefs, the next step is to challenge them and reframe them in a positive light. This can involve examining the evidence for and against each belief, and asking yourself whether it is really true. For example, if you believe that you are not good at public speaking, you might ask yourself whether you have any evidence to support this belief, such as past experiences where you were successful in public speaking or received positive feedback.

In addition to challenging self-limiting beliefs, it is also important to replace them with positive, empowering beliefs that support your goals and aspirations. This can involve creating affirmations and positive self-talk that counter the negative beliefs, and focusing on your strengths and achievements. For example, if you believe that you are not good at public speaking, you might repeat affirmations like "I am a confident and effective public speaker" and focus on instances where you have successfully delivered presentations or speeches.

Another effective strategy for overcoming self-limiting beliefs is to surround yourself with supportive people who believe in you and your abilities. This might involve seeking out a mentor or coach who can provide encouragement and guidance, or finding a support group of like-minded individuals who are working towards similar goals. When you have people in your life who believe in you and encourage you, it becomes easier to believe in yourself and overcome any self-doubt or negative thoughts.

Finally, it is important to practice self-care and engage in activities that promote personal growth and well-being. This might involve setting aside time for self-reflection and introspection, engaging in physical exercise or mindfulness practices, and seeking out new experiences and challenges that help you to grow and develop. When you are taking care of yourself and pursuing your goals with a positive attitude, it becomes easier to overcome self-limiting beliefs and make positive choices that lead to success.

Overcoming self-limiting beliefs is a crucial aspect of achieving your goals and leading a fulfilling life. By identifying these beliefs, challenging them, reframing them in a positive light, and engaging in activities that promote personal growth, you can build the confidence and resilience that you need to make positive choices and achieve your aspirations. With the right mindset and approach, anything is possible, and the possibilities for success and fulfillment are truly endless.

*"Believe in yourself and all that you are.
Know that there is something inside you that
is greater than any obstacle."*

෴

III

Setting SMART Goals and Creating a Plan

Goal setting is a powerful tool for achieving success and making positive choices in life. Whether you are looking to make a career change, improve your health, or achieve a personal milestone, setting goals can help you to focus your efforts, stay motivated, and make progress towards your desired outcome. However, not all goals are created equal, and it is important to set goals that are specific, measurable, achievable, relevant, and time-bound in order to maximize your chances of success.

SMART goals are a popular and effective method for setting goals that are focused and achievable. The acronym "SMART" stands for Specific, Measurable, Achievable, Relevant, and Time-bound. When setting a SMART goal, it is important to consider each of these five elements in order to create a goal that is realistic, attainable, and aligned with your priorities.

Specific:

A specific goal is one that is clear, defined, and easy to understand. When setting a goal, it is important to be specific about what you want to achieve, why you want to achieve it, and how you will measure your progress. For example, instead of setting a vague goal like "I want to be healthier," a specific goal might be "I want to lose 10 pounds in the next three months by eating a balanced diet and exercising regularly."

Measurable:

A measurable goal is one that can be quantified and tracked over time. This helps you to monitor your progress and make adjustments as needed in order to stay on track. For example, if your goal is to "lose 10 pounds in the next three months," you can measure your progress by tracking your weight and body fat percentage on a regular basis.

Achievable:

An achievable goal is one that is realistic and within reach, given your current resources, skills, and circumstances. When setting a goal, it is important to consider whether it is attainable given the time and resources that you have available. For example, if you have a demanding job and limited free time, it may not be feasible to set a goal of training for a marathon in the next three months.

Relevant:

A relevant goal is one that is aligned with your values, priorities, and long-term vision for your life. When setting a goal, it is important to consider whether it is important to you and whether it aligns with your overall life goals and aspirations. For example, if your goal is to "lose 10 pounds in the next three months," you might also consider whether this goal is relevant to your overall health and well-being, and whether it aligns with your priorities and values.

Time-bound:

A time-bound goal is one that has a clear deadline or end date. This helps you to focus your efforts and stay motivated, and it also allows you to track your progress over time. For example, if your goal is to "lose 10 pounds in the next three months," you have a clear deadline and end date, which helps you to focus your efforts and stay motivated.

Once you have set your SMART goal, the next step is to create a plan for achieving it. This might involve breaking down your goal into smaller, more manageable steps, identifying the resources that you need to achieve your goal, and setting a timeline for each step. For example, if your goal is to "lose 10 pounds in the next three months," your plan might include steps like "start eating a balanced diet," "exercise for 30 minutes three times a week," and "track your progress and adjust your plan as needed."

In order to stay on track and make progress towards your goal, it is important to regularly review and evaluate your plan. This might involve tracking your progress, making adjustments as needed, and celebrating your successes along the way. Regular self-reflection can help you to identify areas where you may be struggling, and to make changes to your approach in order to overcome any challenges that you may encounter.

In addition to setting SMART goals and creating a plan, there are several other strategies that can help you to achieve your goals and make positive choices. These may include:

Surrounding yourself with supportive people who believe in your goals and will encourage and motivate you along the way.

Staying focused and committed to your goal, even when faced with setbacks or obstacles.

Celebrating your successes, no matter how small, in order to stay motivated and build momentum.

Staying flexible and open to new ideas and opportunities, in order to keep your options open and be ready to take advantage of new opportunities as they arise.

Setting SMART goals and creating a plan is an important step towards achieving your goals and making positive choices in life. By focusing your efforts, staying motivated, and making progress towards your desired outcome, you can build the foundation for a fulfilling and successful life. With hard work, dedication, and the right strategies in place, you can achieve your goals and make a positive impact on the world.

"The only way to make a positive change is
by making positive choices."

IV

Building a Support System for Positive Choices

Building a support system is a crucial aspect of making positive choices and achieving your goals. A support system can help you stay motivated, overcome challenges, and celebrate your successes along the way. Whether it consists of friends, family, a coach, or a mentor, having a strong support system in place can make all the difference in your journey towards success.

One of the first steps in building a support system is identifying the people in your life who are most likely to provide you with the encouragement and motivation you need. This might include close friends and family members who share your values and goals, or individuals who have already achieved success in similar areas of life.

In addition to seeking out supportive individuals, you can also build a support system by joining a community or organization that shares your interests and values. This could include a local sports club, a religious group, or a professional organization related to your field of work. Being part of a community can provide you with a sense of belonging and connection, as well as opportunities to network and learn from others who are on similar journeys.

Having a coach or mentor can also be a valuable part of your support system. A coach or mentor can provide you with guidance and support as you work towards your goals, helping you to stay focused and motivated, and offering insights and advice based on their own experiences. Whether you engage a professional coach, or seek out a mentor in your own life, having someone to turn to for guidance can be a powerful motivator.

Another important aspect of building a support system is developing strong, healthy relationships with the people in your life. This means being open, honest, and supportive with the people you care about, and making an effort to understand their needs and perspectives. When you build strong relationships with others, you can create a network of support that will help you through even the most challenging times.

Building a support system is an essential step towards making positive choices and achieving your goals. Whether it is through seeking out supportive individuals, joining a community, engaging a coach or mentor, or building strong relationships, having a network of support can help you stay focused, motivated, and on track towards success. With the right support system in place, you can take on the world with confidence and achieve your goals.

"*Success is not final, failure is not fatal: it's the courage to continue that counts.*"

ॐ

V
Managing Emotions and Staying Focused

Managing emotions and staying focused are critical components of making positive choices and achieving your goals. Whether you are dealing with stress, anxiety, fear, or frustration, it is important to have strategies in place to help you stay calm and focused, even in the face of challenging circumstances.

One effective way to manage your emotions and stay focused is to engage in regular self-reflection and self-awareness. This might involve setting aside time each day to reflect on your thoughts, feelings, and experiences, and to identify any patterns or themes that emerge. By becoming more aware of your emotional state, you can begin to understand the triggers that lead to negative emotions, and develop strategies for managing these feelings in a healthy and productive way.

In addition to self-reflection, there are several other strategies that can help you to manage your emotions and stay focused, including:

Engaging in regular physical activity, such as exercise, yoga, or meditation, to help you release stress and tension.

Practicing mindfulness and focusing on the present moment, in order to stay calm and focused, even in challenging circumstances.

Seeking support from others, such as a therapist, coach, or support group, in order to work through difficult emotions and gain new insights and perspectives.

Establishing healthy habits, such as eating well, getting enough sleep, and avoiding unhealthy behaviors, such as excessive alcohol consumption, in order to maintain physical and emotional well-being.

In order to stay focused on your goals, it is also important to identify and overcome distractions and temptations that might pull you away from your desired outcome. This might include avoiding time-wasting activities, such as social media or TV, or reducing your exposure to negativity and drama in your life. By staying focused on your goals, you can avoid distractions and stay motivated as you work towards your desired outcome.

Managing emotions and staying focused are critical components of making positive choices and achieving your goals. Whether it is through self-reflection, engaging in physical activity, practicing mindfulness, seeking support, or avoiding distractions, there are many strategies that can help you stay calm, focused, and motivated as you work towards your desired outcome. By taking the time to focus on your emotional well-being, you can build the foundation for a fulfilling and successful life.

"Positive choices lead to positive outcomes."

ജ

VI
Learning from Failure and Moving Forward

Failure is a natural and inevitable part of the journey towards achieving your goals. Despite our best efforts and intentions, we will all experience setbacks, missteps, and missed opportunities along the way. However, it is how we respond to these failures that ultimately determines our success.

The key to learning from failure and moving forward is to embrace a growth mindset and focus on the lessons that can be learned from our experiences. Instead of dwelling on past mistakes or wallowing in disappointment, it is important to approach each failure as an opportunity for growth and improvement. This might involve reflecting on what went wrong, identifying any patterns or tendencies that contributed to the failure, and developing a plan for how to do things differently in the future.

It is also important to cultivate resilience and perseverance in the face of failure. This means accepting that setbacks and obstacles are a natural part of the process, and reframing your perspective to see these experiences as opportunities to learn and grow. By remaining optimistic, focused, and determined, you can maintain your motivation and stay committed to your goals, even in the face of adversity.

In addition, it is important to seek out support and encouragement from others when dealing with failure. Whether it is through friends, family, a support group, or a mentor, having a network of people who believe in you and your abilities can provide the emotional and psychological support you need to keep moving forward.

Ultimately, learning from failure and moving forward is about developing a growth mindset, embracing resilience, and seeking out support and encouragement from others. By focusing on the lessons that can be learned from our experiences, and approaching each setback as an opportunity for growth and improvement, we can stay motivated and committed to our goals, even in the face of adversity.

Failure is a natural and inevitable part of the journey towards achieving your goals, but it is how we respond to these setbacks that ultimately determines our success. By embracing a growth mindset, developing resilience, and seeking out support from others, we can learn from our failures, stay focused on our goals, and ultimately achieve our desired outcome.

☙

"Be the change you wish to see in the world,
and it starts with the choices you make."

&

VII

Building Mental and Physical Strength for Positive Choices

Building mental and physical strength is essential for making positive choices and achieving your goals. A strong mind and body can help you stay focused, motivated, and resilient in the face of challenges and setbacks. Additionally, a healthy lifestyle can improve your overall well-being and increase your chances of success.

To build mental strength, it is important to engage in regular self-reflection, practice mindfulness and meditation, and seek out support and encouragement from others. By developing a positive self-image, cultivating resilience, and seeking out support when needed, you can strengthen your mental and emotional resilience, and be better equipped to handle challenges and setbacks as they arise.

Physical strength, on the other hand, can be achieved through regular exercise and a healthy diet. Engaging in physical activity can improve your overall health and well-being, reduce stress and anxiety, and increase your focus and motivation. A healthy diet, on the other hand, can provide your body with the energy and nutrients it needs to function optimally, helping you to perform at your best.

It is important to find activities and strategies that work for you, and to make self-care a priority. Whether it is through exercise, mindfulness, or spending time with loved ones, make sure to carve out time for yourself and engage in activities that bring you joy and fulfillment.

Building mental and physical strength is essential for making positive choices and achieving your goals. By engaging in regular self-reflection, practicing mindfulness, and seeking out support, as well as engaging in regular exercise and following a healthy diet, you can improve your overall well-being, increase your mental and physical resilience, and be better equipped to handle the challenges and setbacks that come your way. By prioritizing your mental and physical health, you can stay motivated, focused, and committed to your goals, and ultimately achieve the outcomes you desire.

*"Successful people make choices that lead
them to their goals, while unsuccessful people
make excuses."*

જ

VIII

The Power of Positive Thinking and Gratitude

The power of positive thinking and gratitude is a powerful tool for making positive choices and achieving your goals. Positive thinking and gratitude can help you cultivate a positive mindset, reduce stress and anxiety, and increase your overall well-being. Additionally, by focusing on the positive aspects of your life and cultivating a spirit of gratitude, you can improve your resilience and be better equipped to handle challenges and setbacks.

Positive thinking involves reframing negative thoughts and focusing on the positive aspects of your life. This can help you maintain a positive outlook, even in the face of challenges and difficulties. Additionally, by focusing on positive thoughts, you can increase your motivation, energy, and engagement, and be better equipped to tackle your goals and challenges with confidence and determination.

Gratitude, on the other hand, involves recognizing and appreciating the good things in your life. This can help you cultivate a positive outlook and improve your overall well-being. Additionally, by focusing on what you are grateful for, you can reduce stress and anxiety, and increase your overall happiness and satisfaction.

It is important to engage in daily practices that foster positive thinking and gratitude. This can include writing in a gratitude journal, spending time with loved ones, or engaging in mindfulness or meditation. Additionally, seek out opportunities to surround yourself with positive, supportive individuals who will encourage and motivate you along the way.

The power of positive thinking and gratitude is a powerful tool for making positive choices and achieving your goals. By focusing on positive thoughts and cultivating a spirit of gratitude, you can improve your resilience, reduce stress and anxiety, and increase your overall well-being. Additionally, by engaging in daily practices that foster positive thinking and gratitude, you can cultivate a positive mindset and be better equipped to handle challenges and setbacks, ultimately helping you achieve your goals and reach your full potential.

৩

"You are the master of your own destiny, the commander of your own life, the architect of your own future."

ജ

IX

Overcoming Procrastination and Staying Motivated

Procrastination is a common obstacle that can prevent you from making positive choices and achieving your goals. Whether it is due to fear of failure, lack of motivation, or simply being overwhelmed, procrastination can be a major roadblock to success. However, with the right strategies and techniques, you can overcome procrastination and stay motivated in order to achieve your goals.

One key strategy for overcoming procrastination is to break down large goals into smaller, more manageable tasks. By focusing on smaller, achievable steps, you can avoid feeling overwhelmed and keep yourself motivated to continue making progress. Additionally, it is important to prioritize your tasks and focus on the most important ones first. This can help you stay focused and avoid getting sidetracked by less important tasks.

Another effective technique for overcoming procrastination is to set deadlines and hold yourself accountable. This can help you stay focused and motivated, as well as keep you on track towards achieving your goals. Additionally, it is important to establish a routine and stick to it as much as possible. This can help you develop good habits and create a structure for your day-to-day life that supports your goals.

Staying motivated is another important aspect of overcoming procrastination and achieving your goals. This can be done by celebrating your successes, setting rewards for yourself, and surrounding yourself with supportive individuals who will encourage and motivate you along the way. Additionally, it is important to maintain a positive attitude and focus on the progress you are making, rather than dwelling on setbacks or failures.

Overcoming procrastination and staying motivated are critical components of making positive choices and achieving your goals. By breaking down large goals into smaller, manageable tasks, setting deadlines and holding yourself accountable, and staying motivated and positive, you can overcome procrastination and keep yourself on track towards achieving your goals. With dedication and commitment, you can unlock the secrets to making positive choices and reach your full potential.

"A goal without a plan is just a wish."

જી

X

Building Positive Choices in the Face of Adversity

Adversity is a natural part of life and can come in many forms, from personal struggles and setbacks to larger, societal challenges. Despite these difficulties, it is possible to build positive choices even in the face of adversity. By using the right strategies and techniques, you can cultivate resilience and maintain a positive outlook, even in the most challenging of circumstances.

One key strategy for building positive choices in the face of adversity is to focus on what you can control. This means shifting your focus away from things that you cannot change, such as the past or external circumstances, and instead, focusing on things that you can control, such as your thoughts, feelings, and actions. By focusing on what you can control, you can avoid feeling overwhelmed and maintain a sense of agency in the face of adversity.

Another effective technique for building positive choices in the face of adversity is to cultivate a growth mindset. A growth mindset is the belief that you can grow, learn, and develop in the face of challenges and difficulties. By embracing a growth mindset, you can view adversity as an opportunity to learn and grow, rather than as a threat to your success and well-being.

In addition to these strategies, it is important to build a support system of positive and supportive individuals who can help you navigate adversity. Whether it is friends, family, or a professional counselor, having a strong support system can provide you with the encouragement, motivation, and guidance you need to make positive choices and overcome adversity.

Finally, it is important to take care of your mental and physical health in the face of adversity. This can include engaging in physical exercise, practicing self-care, and developing healthy coping mechanisms, such as meditation or journaling. By taking care of your mental and physical health, you can build resilience and maintain a positive outlook, even in the most challenging of circumstances.

Building positive choices in the face of adversity is a critical component of achieving your goals. By focusing on what you can control, cultivating a growth mindset, building a support system, and taking care of your mental and physical health, you can cultivate resilience and maintain a positive outlook, even in the face of adversity. With determination and perseverance, you can overcome any obstacle and achieve your goals.

"The choices you make today will determine
the path you will follow tomorrow."

⇢

XI

The Importance of Self-Care for Making Positive Choices

Self-care is a critical component of making positive choices and achieving your goals. It involves taking the time to care for your physical, mental, and emotional health and well-being, so that you are able to function at your best. Without self-care, it can be difficult to make positive choices and sustain the motivation and focus needed to achieve your goals.

One of the primary benefits of self-care is that it helps you manage stress and reduce burnout. In today's fast-paced world, stress levels are often high, and it can be tempting to push yourself too hard in an effort to achieve your goals. However, this can lead to burnout, which can have a negative impact on your health and well-being. By engaging in self-care activities, such as exercise, relaxation, and spending time with loved ones, you can reduce stress and prevent burnout, allowing you to maintain a positive outlook and make positive choices.

Self-care can also help you build resilience in the face of adversity. Resilience is the ability to bounce back from setbacks and challenges, and it is a critical component of achieving your goals. By engaging in self-care activities, you can build resilience, helping you to recover more quickly from setbacks and maintain a positive outlook, even in the face of adversity.

In addition, self-care can help you build a positive mindset and cultivate gratitude. A positive mindset is the foundation of making positive choices, and self-care can help you maintain a positive outlook, even in the face of adversity. By engaging in self-care activities that you enjoy, such as meditation, journaling, or spending time in nature, you can cultivate gratitude and appreciate the good things in your life, even in the most challenging of circumstances.

Finally, self-care can help you maintain good physical and mental health, which is critical for achieving your goals. By engaging in self-care activities that promote physical and mental well-being, such as exercise, healthy eating, and adequate sleep, you can maintain good physical and mental health, allowing you to make positive choices and achieve your goals.

Self-care is an essential component of making positive choices and achieving your goals. By reducing stress, building resilience, cultivating a positive mindset, and maintaining good physical and mental health, you can make positive choices and sustain the motivation and focus needed to achieve your goals. By taking care of yourself, you can achieve your goals and live a fulfilling life.

"You are not defined by your past, you are
defined by the choices you make today."

ღ

XII

Learning to Adapt and Be Flexible

Making positive choices and achieving your goals can be a challenging journey, but it's important to understand that setbacks and obstacles are a natural part of the process. The ability to adapt and be flexible in the face of adversity is a key factor in success.

One of the biggest challenges people face when trying to achieve their goals is the need to change their behavior and thinking patterns. This can be difficult, as our brains are wired to resist change. But learning to adapt and be flexible can help you overcome these obstacles and achieve your goals.

To begin, it's important to understand the importance of being open-minded and receptive to new ideas and experiences. This means being willing to try new approaches and be open to feedback from others.

Additionally, it's important to have a growth mindset, where you believe that you have the ability to improve and grow, and that setbacks and failures are simply opportunities for learning and growth.

Another key aspect of being flexible and adaptable is being able to handle stress and uncertainty. When faced with a difficult situation, it's important to stay calm and focused, and to use effective stress-management techniques to help you cope. This could include mindfulness, meditation, or exercise.

It's also important to be flexible in your goal setting. While having specific goals can be helpful, it's also important to be willing to adjust your plans as needed. This might mean adjusting your timeline, changing your approach, or even altering your goals altogether if circumstances change.

Finally, it's important to embrace change and be willing to pivot when necessary. This means being open to new opportunities, taking calculated risks, and being willing to try new things.

Being flexible and adaptable is a critical component of making positive choices and achieving your goals. By being open-minded, having a growth mindset, handling stress effectively, being flexible in your goal setting, and embracing change, you'll be well on your way to success. Remember, the journey to achieving your goals is not a straight line, but by being flexible and adaptable, you'll be able to navigate the ups and downs and come out on top.

&

"*Life is a series of choices, make the right
ones and you'll have no regrets.*"

XIII

The Role of Mindfulness in Making Positive Choices

Mindfulness is a mental state achieved by focusing one's awareness on the present moment, while calmly acknowledging and accepting one's feelings, thoughts, and bodily sensations. This mental state has been shown to have a number of benefits for individuals looking to make positive choices and achieve their goals.

One of the main benefits of mindfulness is that it helps to reduce stress and anxiety. When individuals are feeling overwhelmed and stressed, it can be difficult to make positive choices and stay focused on their goals. By practicing mindfulness, individuals can learn to recognize when they are feeling stressed and take steps to manage their emotions more effectively.

Mindfulness can also help individuals to become more self-aware. This self-awareness can then be used to identify negative patterns of behavior and thought that are limiting their progress towards their goals. For example, an individual may realize that they often become discouraged when faced with a challenge and that this tendency is holding them back. By recognizing this pattern, they can take steps to change their approach and make more positive choices.

In addition to improving self-awareness, mindfulness can also help individuals to develop better focus and concentration. When we are mindful, we are able to focus our attention on the present moment and avoid getting distracted by irrelevant thoughts and distractions. This ability to focus can be incredibly valuable when working to achieve long-term goals.

Finally, mindfulness can also help individuals to develop greater resilience in the face of adversity. By learning to be present and aware in the moment, individuals can learn to accept setbacks and challenges as an opportunity for growth and learning, rather than becoming discouraged and giving up. This resilience can be a key factor in helping individuals to stay motivated and make positive choices over the long-term.

In order to get the most out of mindfulness, it is important to practice regularly. This can involve setting aside time each day for mindfulness meditation, practicing mindful breathing exercises, or simply taking a few moments throughout the day to focus on the present moment and your thoughts and feelings.

Mindfulness is an incredibly powerful tool for individuals looking to make positive choices and achieve their goals. By developing greater self-awareness, improving focus and concentration, and building resilience in the face of adversity, individuals can use mindfulness to stay motivated and on track towards their goals. So, make mindfulness a part of your daily routine and start experiencing the benefits today.

"Small positive choices lead to big positive changes."

ₔ

XIV

The Power of Persistence and Determination

Making positive choices and achieving our goals can be a challenging process that requires a lot of effort and dedication. However, the most successful individuals have one common trait: they are persistent and determined. They have the drive to overcome obstacles and keep pushing forward, no matter how difficult the journey may be.

Persistence and determination are key components of success. It's the ability to keep going, even when things seem impossible, that sets the high-achievers apart from the rest. When faced with setbacks and challenges, the persistent and determined individual will find a way to keep moving forward, whereas others may give up or lose their motivation.

To be persistent and determined, it's important to have a strong sense of purpose and a clear understanding of your goals. When you know what you want, you're more likely to stay focused and motivated, even when faced with obstacles. Additionally, it's crucial to develop a positive attitude and have faith in your abilities. Believing in yourself and your abilities can help you stay motivated and overcome challenges with ease.

It's also essential to be patient and recognize that success takes time. Many individuals give up too soon because they expect immediate results. However, success is a journey, not a destination. It takes time, effort, and persistence to achieve your goals. It's essential to understand that setbacks are a normal part of the process and that they should be seen as opportunities for growth and learning.

One of the most significant benefits of being persistent and determined is that it helps to build resilience. Resilience is the ability to bounce back from setbacks and keep moving forward. It's a crucial component of success and allows individuals to overcome obstacles and reach their goals.

Another important aspect of persistence and determination is having a growth mindset. A growth mindset is the belief that you can learn, grow, and improve. It's about embracing challenges as opportunities for growth and seeing setbacks as opportunities for learning and improvement.

Persistence and determination are crucial components of success. They help individuals overcome obstacles, stay motivated, and achieve their goals. To be persistent and determined, it's essential to have a strong sense of purpose, a clear understanding of your goals, a positive attitude, and a growth mindset. By embracing these traits, you can achieve your goals and make positive choices that lead to a successful and fulfilling life.

"The secret to success is to keep making
positive choices."

ॐ

XV

Making Positive Choices to Achieve Your Goals

Finally, setting and achieving goals requires a combination of clear planning, hard work, and positive decision making. It's important to start by defining specific, measurable, and attainable goals, and creating a step-by-step plan to reach them. To stay motivated, you can break your goals into smaller, manageable tasks and celebrate your progress along the way. Making positive choices and avoiding negative behaviors, such as procrastination or self-doubt, can also help you stay on track and reach your full potential. By putting all these elements together, you can increase your chances of success and achieve your goals.

"The future is created by the choices you make today."

"Don't wait for opportunity, create it through the choices you make."

"The key to happiness is making positive choices that align with your values."

"When faced with a choice, choose to make the right one, even if it's the harder one."

"Positive choices lead to a positive life."

"Success is not a destination, it's a journey made up of the choices you make"

೮౩

OTHER BOOKS OF THE AUTHOR

1. The Moments When I Met God
2. Kashiyile Theertha Pathangal
3. GURU GYAN VANI
4. Abhiprerak Gita
5. ASSI SE JAIN GHAT TAK
6. Hopelessness of Arjuna
7. The Soul and It's True Nature
8. Sense of Action (Karma)
9. Action through Wisdom
10. Action through Wisdom
11. THEORY AND PRACTICAL OF EVERY ACTION
12. LOGICAL UNDERSTANDING OF THE SUPREME
13. THE IMPERISHABLE SUPREME
14. Yatra Nishadraj se Hanuman Ghat Tak
15. Yatra Karnatak Ghat se Raja Ghat Tak
16. Yatra Pandey Ghat se Prayagraj Ghat Tak
17. Yatra Ranjendra Prasad Ghat se Dattatreya Ghat Tak
18. YaatraSindhiya Ghat se Gwaliar Ghat Tak
19. Yatra Mangala Gauri Ghat se Hanuman Gadhi Ghat Tak
20. Yatra Gaay Ghat Se Nishad Ghat Tak
21. MAA GANGA, GHATEN EVM UTSAV
22. Ganga Arti Dev Deepavali evam Any Utsav
23. Potentials of Digitalized India
24. VEDIC CONSCIOUSNESS
25. A Brief Introduction to Vedic Science
26. Kashi ke Barah Jyotirling
27. IMPACT OF MOTIVATION
28. Let's have a Milky Way Journey
29. Color Therapy in a Nutshell

CONTACT

DR. JAGADEESH PILLAI

MBA & PhD in Vedic Science

Four Times Guinness World Record Holder

Winner of Mahatma Gandhi Vishwa Shanti Puraskar and
Global Peace Ambassador

Gemology, Astro & Vastu Consultant - Spiritual Counselor

Consultant for designing World Record Ideas

Efficient Tarot Card Reader

9839093003

myrichindia@gmail.com

drjagadeeshpillai@facebook

drjagadeeshpillai@instagram
jagadeeshpillai@youtube

www. JAGADEESHPILLAI.com

৵

|| LOKAHA SAMASTHAHA SUKHINO BHAVANTU ||

ॐ